Other books by Mark Allen Gray ...

The Hounds of Love

Embedded in America

The House of Man

and other works under construction.

I0190539

Gray Technologies Press

Rocking
in a Free World

Rocking in a Free World

by
Mark Allen Gray

Gray Technologies Press

Rocking in a Free World

Published 2006 by
Gray Technologies Press
Bel Air, Maryland, United States of America
www.graytechpress.com

Library of Congress Control Number: 2004096581

ISBN 0-9761095-3-0

Printed in the United States of America.

Revision Number 2006.12.07.41

Gray Technologies Press

Dedication

This book is dedicated to the Committee of Five of the Second Continental Congress of the Thirteen United States of America.

Contents

Introduction

Rocking in a Free World is a collection of poems about freedom. Like love, the subject of the author's previous work, freedom is a fundamental human experience with many levels of abstraction and interpretation. Unlike love, freedom transcends the bonds of interpersonal relationships providing a catalyst for the formation of societies, cultures, religions, governments, and nations. All societies, regardless of size, can be measured by the freedoms they cultivate for their citizens.

Whether we want to or not, we all participate in freedom and measure our worthiness in our respective societies by the degree that we adhere to our allowed freedom. In a virgin world, there are no rules, no boundaries of action, expression, or responsibility – complete freedom. But a world without rules, without boundaries, is a world in chaos and destined to extinction. Some level of conformance is required to sustain any society. By the basic need of survival, to propagate the species, we construct rules, consider them, express them, try them, reject them, hold them, argue them, embrace them, and celebrate them.

This book is organized into four chapters of poems on the subjects of independence, journey, struggle, and celebration. Freedom cannot exist without the free will of independent thought. Independence cultivates freedom that in turn can be molded by its participants into whatever society they collectively embrace, either by will or by force. Journey is required for evolution, adaptation and growth. Journey will challenge the rules of your freedom and make you consider and embrace change for the sake of sustainability. Struggle is inevitable and constant. Struggle results in conflict, imprisonment, revolution, war, and change. Wars are fought over disparate views of freedom and battles are lost, won, and celebrated. These conflicts occur at so many levels within and between societies, but in all cases there is celebration of the victories through art. Art is the apex of the celebration of freedom.

In our modern world, Rock music is a widely embraced pure artistic expression of freedom. The art of Rock is centered first on the individual and their capacity to express themselves freely, without social, religious, or political persecution. Secondly, Rock music expresses the artist's capacity to share and integrate their expression with others to create a rhythm in lyric, sound, and vision. These components combined, can create a force that will shake souls and change the world without war. Radio Free Europe is a testament to the power of freedom of speech. Suppression breeds contempt that thirsts for art and change. A wall that formed an iron curtain fell. The fundamental right of freedom is unstoppable. The free pen of expression is mightier than the slave sword of silence.

On September 11, 2001 the world witnessed the price of freedom in a single blow to the superpower that loves its freedom. It was a blow directly to the heart of freedom's economic icon on the edge of freedom's borders. It was, without a doubt, a bold and calculated blow intended to make a big statement. And it was heard. And the giant of freedom no longer sleeps or dreams the sweet dream, the American dream. The giant is troubled and insecure. This is a doubled-edged sword. One edge sliced American security and the other edge slashes back in defense. America is no longer a slumbering brute of tolerance and pride; America is on a war path. America's citizens, public servants, law makers, policy makers, teachers, mothers, fathers, sons, daughters, its war fighters, and its peace makers are awake and strong. America is divided and the world is divided. But freedom will heal these wounds and the world will be stronger for it.

Perhaps one day, entire worlds or even clusters of worlds will be defined by the measure of their unified freedom, balancing the greatest level of peace against the least loss of life, for a collective and sustainable future of humanity and coexistence with unstoppable compassion and love of life.

Each chapter in this book begins with a graphic symbol. These symbols are a creation of the author. Through human history, similar graphical forms have been used by diverse cultures to symbolize similar ideas. In all cases the idea is encapsulated in a circle (a "life" circle), a commonly used symbol in Celtic culture. Each circle comprises three layers representing birth, life, and death. The content of each circle defines the idea expressed by that chapter.

The first chapter on Independence is represented by a life circle encompassing a letter A. This represents the force of anarchy on our birth/life/death existence. Encircling anarchy with life and purpose gives it form that creates independence.

The second chapter on Journey is represented by a life circle encompassing the four major rose lines of the compass, north, south, east, and west. The compass symbol is universal and journey is a key component to the spread of our human ideas around our world.

The third chapter on Struggle is represented by a life circle encompassing two arrows in opposing directions reflected about a vertical axis. In all major conflict at the personal or social level there are typically two major opposing forces, either in debate or battle. The two arrows represent the conflict resulting from individuals and cultures clashing in their efforts to secure their ideologies.

The fourth chapter on Celebration is represented by a life circle encompassing a solid circle. The solid circle represents a seed of common understanding resulting from the journey through independence and struggle. The seed planted and cultivated is destined to nourish future generations.

Completing the symbology of this book is a symbol formed by composing the four chapter symbols into one new symbol. The resulting composite of the symbols of Independence, Journey, Struggle, and Celebration is the symbol of Freedom.

In a world of free will, freedom is a priceless natural resource without ownership. Freedom is a natural right of each one of us. *Rocking in a Free World* combines various elements of artistic expression with historical bearing and recent global events in a poetic articulation of the development towards pure freedom in a human context as we know it now. We have a long way to go. This is simply a snapshot in time.

"There's colors on the street
Red, white and blue
People shufflin' their feet
People sleepin' in their shoes
But there's a warnin' sign
on the road ahead
There's a lot of people sayin'
we'd be better off dead
Don't feel like Satan,
but I am to them
So I try to forget it,
any way I can.
Keep on rockin' in the free world"

— Neil Young

Chapter One:
Independence

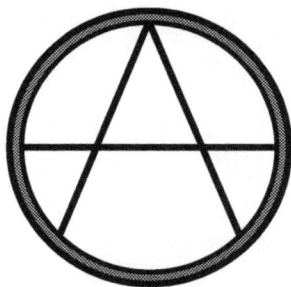

Gagged and Bound

Civilization feeds

On old money wisdom

And young ambition

Isolation for those without

The river isn't free

It's a slave to gravity

Worth

Independence is a treasure
Sunk deep in a ship
Off the shore of freedom's golden coast
The cats of electric strings
Resurrect the song of ghost days
Spinning tales of anarchy on the seas
Of modern man in search of old value
Heavy metal megalomaniacs
Burn through gigantic sound
In extreme attempts to connect to the dead
And disconnect themselves from the masses
Of man burdened by modern vice and virtue
The voice of independent thought is tricky
In new windows of commercial success
A dark Sabbath is observed one day
And celebrated in convenience and profit
On the morrow
What treasure is worth a life?

Tunneling

A beautiful smile
Can stay for awhile
A dangerous move
Can shine for a mile

In the security of trust
The sense of want
To be in the know
Of great secrets grow

Tunnel through
Slip by the guards
Into the midnight
Cloaked and scarred

Six Senses

Hear it now
The loud sound of bright daylight
See it now
The sampled images of thunder rolling

Smell it now
The sharp odor of bitter words
Taste it now
The odd flavor stinks of deception

Feel it now
The warm touch of true faith
Believe it now
Unconditional faith in the palm of your hand

The tools of mortality
That realize existence
Create a sixth sense
When freed from convention

Evolver

Independence is a catalyst for evolution

Music is a drug
That shakes, rocks, and rolls
That jazzes the brain
And hits your blues in the head
That rolls through your cells
Injects its essence into your soul
Music is a force of nature
An art form of self expression

Freedom is a goal
Of every cell that lives
And multiplies
In the ether

The watch tower watches
And the Tower towers
Over the mass of men
That lead quiet lives
In outrageous times

Psychedelic visions of reality
Are pathetic attempts
To understand other worlds
While we create weapons
Of mass destruction
And position them on the board

What question do we pose

7

To the creator that creates
A pause
That gives us time to react?

Is there any question
That has no answer?
Is there any intelligence
That has all of the answers?
What history of human existence
Does not have questions
That cannot be answered?

The heart beats now and now and now and
now and now ...
As required by DNA

The soul cries, weeps, jumps, sleeps, and
rejoices
In the faith of religion

Manhood cringes and throbs
Sex in the cells

Evolution is real

One Percenters

Gasoline
Oil
Grease
And fear

Chopped bikes
Another run
Outlaw down in the street
Sent home to mother
In a box

Big news
Gang rape
Suburbia hungers
For dinner entertainment
Truth dissolved in media frenzy

No love for law
Nothing to lose
Bound only by the colors
And a common lust for freedom
Man, machine, road, and sky

American children of a world at war
Loosened on a modern wild west

Blood
Booze
Semen
And tears

Vineyard

Words of hope clinging
Like wet leaves to dead logs
Jammed in the spring tide's ebb
A vineyard awash is dead

Words tumble and fall
Spinning and reeling
The toilet vortex sucking hope
Into the cesspool

Clinging to the vine
The wine is impossible
In the master's hand
The grape is wine

Freedom forms in strange crystals
Large with time
Small in the moment
Always present

In the vineyard
Imagine the possibilities
And infinite forms
The savior's passion
To restore the order
Lost in the garden

One World

The cosmic wheel whirs
To the pop beat
Small and strange
In this phantasmic mix of disjointed cultures
Coagulating into a giant question mark
Probing the perfection
Of a world in oneness

I love my freedom
I know about selfish freedom
I am free to love
I know about selfless love

Once there was one
Then there were two
Now there are too many
Lost in love wanting freedom

One world
One life
One you

The Savage Earth

The savage Earth presents itself
To the ether glow of the moon
Surrendering in the autumn of the season
A harvest of summer's sun
Lifeless products for consumption

The government of the instant swells
And bursts when time stands still
The scene must change
Always
Or we will die

Do you remember
Life in the dream's eye storm
A world without fire
Dark and cold
A world before Grandmother Spider?

The house is cold without a fire
Build it well
Make it well
Dare to dream
A window on past and future

Touch the rock
Feel the roll
Make peace with the savage Earth
The womb of humanity
Freedom under gravity

Freedom Flag

Freedom is a new day
A cloud
A stray
A new way
Great freedom, burning flag

Freedom is a flag burning bright
Proclaiming first amendment right
Kill the flame, stake your claim
Get your freedom another name

I would never burn a flag
Say they're wrong, call them fags
I believe in ideals
In freedom's existential wheels

To hell with burning flags
I proclaim an old ideal
Let it be!

The Golden Expression

The golden expression of man
Buried deep in secret places
Creates a power of want
What drive makes us seek
The pure element
Of our planet's treasure
Pirates sail the seas
And sacrifice their lives
To behold and hold its essence
Blood shed bled
In desperate attempts
To feel the grace of the metal
That defines kingdoms
And betrays our love of life
A man measured in pure gold
Is a ghost of salvation
A beggar measured in good deeds
Is a savior of our faith
Why do we seek wealth
But for power over our neighbor
A benchmark of material progression
When our infinite soul struggles
To be real in our sad existence
Our grace is the gold to behold

The politician takes to the podium
What vices does he pander to,
What enemies of our freedom
Does he conjure up to destroy?

A babe cries from simple want
A child complains for wisdom
A young man screams for independence
An old man yearns for youth

The summer night has many voices
Insects create a buzz and a hum
Competing with the birds that
Have ended their hunt of the day
As if to proclaim their victory
Frogs make so many sounds
Leaping from pond to tree
From the deep of the bull frog
To the heights of the tree frog
To the silence of the giant oaks
That sway and shudder
Their leaves in the summer night breeze

While the Doppler effect
Of passing vehicles
Stroke the evening canvas
Chirp, hum, buzz, and rush
Asynchronously define and create
A symphony of the night

The comedy of the day multiplies
As the night progresses
Making big laughter
A harmless irony is magnified
By the night's humor
Fueled by alcohol's need for laughter
The pale reality of the day
Transforms into laughter

Of the night

Sometimes I am unhappy
Of the portrayal of time
And sometimes I am wild
With the irony of the day

Wild secrets try to escape me
Only to be squashed by myself
What catalyst is required
To release them?

I am a clown in a circus
Juggling ideas
One fall and I hurt
Deeply

Beyond Us

I think therefore I am
I feel therefore I love
We are thinkers and lovers
We are human

What forms of life exist in this universe?
Do they think?
Do they feel?
Do they do something greater or lesser
Than thinking or feeling?

What other forms of existence are there
Than thinking and feeling?
Are we smug in our limitations?
Full and righteous?

A cell divides
A thought considers
What other forms could be
Beyond our limited capacity?

The Prisoner

The prisoner, a repeat offender
Fears himself, his freedom
Grabs hold, makes his crime
The prisoner reenters the prison

Kill the father, authority
Enter the mother, prison
Oedipus at large in America
Filling our prisons

Free will is great responsibility
More than the prisoner can suffer
Loss of freedom relieves the pain
Secures the shelter of the womb

The prisoner reenters the prison
Into the safety
Into the cave
Into the abyss that belched him into existence

A vicious cycle
Can be broken in song

Probation Ends

Sitting in the waiting room of the processing office of the motor vehicle administration of this great state of our great country, I wait to remove the restriction on my driver's license. Two years ago I screwed up. That's another story. For a time I lost my driving privilege. For the remaining days I've been marked with the black spot of driving restriction, a fateful mark should I be pulled over with any evidence of foul play coursing through my veins; another trial and jail time for sure. But I have struggled and I have won and I am free again. Free to error and free to overcome. Free of the threat of urban cowboy lynching posse lights in the rear view mirror. Never free of the dreams that haunt me. Probation ends, independence begins again.

Chapter Two:
Journey

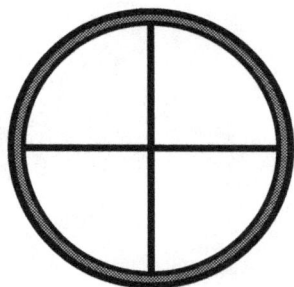

The Hill

Jack and Jim went up the hill

To fetch a pail of wisdom.

Jack fell down and broke his crown

And Jim went stumbling with him.

Starship

Eyes squeezed shut
Linger on one color
That fades into black and blue
Blur

Uncertainty is certain
Probability is certain
Together they dance
And make days

Sunshine drives
Moonshine reflects
Starshine wanders
The distance of galaxies
And enters pores
Mingles with psyche
Creates vision
In a desert of reason

A Heart of Gold
Is a pirate's prize
A great big reason
To travel the skies

A starship enters
A galaxy today
With no agenda
And no game to play

Explorer

I am an explorer
Wrapped in flesh, bone, and blood
Stewed in hope, faith, and religion
Swirling in a pot of capitalism, democracy, and
mediocrity
So many tasty stews on the stove

When Fate consumes me
Like a pill in the belly of hunger
The layers of culture dissolve
Releasing a kernel of existence
To explore the bowels of infinity

The Ocean

The womb of the our planet Earth
Is the Ocean
In the humdrum of our terrestrial lives
We seek it.

What force draws the mass of humanity
To gamble hard earned time
For a splash in the surf
For salt in the wounds of our being?

Is there an angel for each of us
That wonders the same wonder
That watches over our sins
Committed to our pilgrimage?

A parting of the great waters
Is not an option
That fits our present situation
Freedom is inherited and assumed.

The Ocean is a pleasant comfort
That seeks and destroys
In chaotic oblivion
Of our individualism.

We often take comfort
In our science of reason
And fail to take faith
In our basic need to believe.

Over America

One day I flew across America
A sunny Spring day
From east to west
Over sleepy freedom

The pilot offered a tour
Of the Grand Canyon
Dipping hard to the right
At 36000 feet

Billions of years unfolded
Beneath our bellies
In a blue sky
Shadows evidence of relief

The creatures responded
In curiosity
Wonders of the world
Confident in destiny

The engines roared on
As expected
The creatures relaxed
In security

Tiny worlds colliding beneath
For a while with God
Invincible
And sure

The Parade

The cars crawl by
A soft parade
Rain or shine
Vacations made

Small imports
Hip-hop beats
A time for fun
Where people meet

S-U-Vs
With big shiny rims
4-by-4s
Hell bent on sin

Muscle cars
Rumble and squeal
Guido mobiles
Hunt for meals

Chaos contained
And channeled by tar
Funneled to a vanishing point
The bars

Inhibitions lay bare
Consumed by alcohol
The parade without end
Never stalls

On a Rocket

The hip hop
It don't stop
The planet rock
It's a sure shot

My foot, it shake
My hip, it break
My soul, it roll, it rock, it sing
I'm on a rocket

Can't stop it

The Highlands

Through heather, fern, birch, and moor
We pass
Pilgrims on a journey

Ancient castle ruins
Tales of princess tolls
And great ships
And Viking games

These hills are old
Where Macbeth bones lay
Misty covered firths and lochs
Harboring tales of maidens
And kelpies

The mountains are crying
Awash in tears
Where tall forests of spruce
Sheltered McKenzies and MacDonalds
In futile thirst of pride's avenging grip

Letting go to Moorish haunts
Exposing the bones
In capricious cairns
Strath and glen were divided
In a single ice age

Long before the time
Of Vikings, Celts, and Clans

Galilee

Early spring, desert night
Traveling twentieth century roads
Over first century footpaths
To the sea
U.N. trucks pass
We roll on
From high desert mountain holy place
Nazareth

Tiberias
On the sea of Galilee
Descending, switching, rolling on down
Down to the sea
The lights consume
And we are taken
Into the belly of the city

The city sleeps
But not the shore
Markets, merchants, good deals, fresh fish
"Sit down, we have the best!"
An outdoor café and a plate of St. Peter's fish
A warm cappuccino and a cool sea breeze

Arabian disco boats
Aglow and booming
Big beats from shore to shore
The big boats
Crawling like hungry sea monsters
Palestine dancing to the frantic music

In Friday night freedom and disdain
Giving it to the night

A view of the Golan Heights
Outlined by the lights of settlements
On the shore
Border guards hanging out
Some dancing with guns overhead
Shaken in mindless contempt

Others aloof and aware

Hair

I asked myself one day,
"Am I really free, or am I a prisoner of
convention?"

And my soul began to weep
A tear formed on the back of my head

Gilgamesh wandering the desert
Lamenting the loss of innocence

The Land of Enchantment

New Mexico Tech 1979. Post disco burnout and neo-country revival. Central American war and the Iran hostage crisis. Hi-tech on the horizon. Rock scene disjointed – classic/disco/punk/metal. Pink Floyd ("How can you have any pudding, if you don't eat your meat?"). Lots-O-Pot and the Mushroom Man. Fantasy games – Middle Earth – Dungeons & Dragons. Close encounters with a bad bunch. No TV. Gas money is gold and freedom. Buying underage. Rock climbing. Mining. Cross country skiing. Turtle Bay. Panning for gold. Staurolite crystals – Earth bleeding crucifix. Pink hearts, black beauties, and all nighters. Townies & Techies. St. Patrick's day escape in Taos Canyon. Street racing in ABQ. Headers, regular gas, and oil changes (the oil back into the desert – cycles!). Christmas vacation and the trip home. Summer vacation and the trip home. The trip back. The smell of the desert after a rain. Roasting chilies and chili cook-offs. Geology field trips and Friday afternoons. Thanksgiving. The brownie incident. Searching for girls; Candy-O. The food poisoning incident. The stop sign incident. The desert night sky and the Milky Way. Lonely times and drives – missing family. Academic pressure – competition – and the almighty GPA. Socorro.

The Boardwalk

How many streets terminate
Breathing life
Into this structure that winds and plots
Along the shore just out of reach
Of the tides that ebb and flow
From day to day and year to year

As lives change, grow and fade
And move forward
And sometimes trip and fall
The boardwalk stays and lives on

Consider a day
That life triumphs and death dies
The ocean offering a gift
Laid out at the feet of coastal attempts
To define a boundary
Between man and big nature

Just off shore Dolphins on cruise control
Give a glimpse of other streets
To coastal highways on the other side

Summer's End

The summer's over

We swam in the ocean
And played in the waves
Walked on the boardwalk
And played those same games

Whack-A-Mole
And Blast-A-Monkey
Galaga
And anything funky

Got the picture
Got the fries
Got the chocolate covered banana
No lies

Thanksgiving Prayer

I remember that Thanksgiving Day
At the beach
In the Bahamas

It was cool sweet soft and gentle
The breeze the air
The sun hot pure and driven
Animating the sea in a liquid texture
Of diamonds and emeralds

Boats dancing, racing, crashing
Through the crystal sunshine
Children intense on sand fortresses
And creations of the moment while the
Surf beats, and beats, and beats a rhythm

A clock, a synchronization, a signal
A heartbeat of the Earth
The wind pulling huge vaporous clouds
Through a deep dome of blue in a sky

And the Earth mass pulled us down
In a comfortable sense of belonging
In a naïve knowledge that this
Is what is supposed to be
Unaware that this is simply what happened

I give thanks to this happening
To this day, to yesterday, to tomorrow
Amen

Constant Motion

More than 14 billion years after the Big Bang, which was the beginning of our known Universe, there is in this Universe of billions of galaxy clusters, a single galaxy cluster of billions of galaxies. And in this galaxy cluster of billions of galaxies, there is this one galaxy of billions of stars. And in this galaxy of billions of stars there is this one star with nine or 10 planets, more or less. And on this single planet that circles this one star of billions of stars in a galaxy that is one of billions of galaxies in one galaxy cluster that is one cluster of billions of galaxy clusters in this Universe there is one person that is you. And you are one of over six billion people suffering your suffer every day as this planet spins another spin on its axis. And as the planet spins another spin about its star, and as the star spins another spin about its galaxy, and as the galaxy spins another spin about its cluster, and as the cluster spins another spin through the great void of the Universe, and as the Universe spins on its axis, being a spec of dust on the ceiling fan in the creator's bedroom, we ride while she sleeps and spins dreams. And the constant motions continue on their predictable paths through eternity.

What if all motion in the Universe ceased? Would the Universe cease to exist? Its existence defined only by constant motion and the resulting Physics? Is it even possible to measure all of the vectors of motion that we fly through each moment relative to some cosmic focal point? No mater our free will. What act of man could change any of this? Perhaps it is just an illusion. One day this tiny planet will meet its fate in a collision path that was pre-determined at the instant of the Big Bang. Is the Universe a constant or a variable? I challenge mankind to alter the Big Bang's pre-determined paths. Only then will we be truly free. In the meantime, enjoy your illusion on this wild ride.

Chapter Three:
Struggle

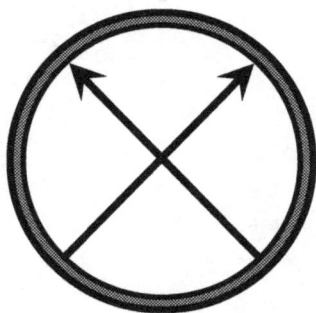

Inner Daemons

Eyes open that do not see
Bent on a hell within the soul
Waging a war on the daemons
That never sleep

A slow death in the afternoon
Creates synaptic connections that live
When transposed to art
And breathed to life in the witching hours

Pretty faces with ugly souls dance
Synchronized to the will of madness
A contradiction of terms
And a comfy retreat for remorse

Tell me your name strange one
Syd you say?
Have we met before?
Your sound is familiar

A dream is psychedelic and abstract
And we wake and understand
But a psychosis is real and disturbing
Ironically with the dark side in the sun

The daemons are relentless psycho robots
Probing our sensory system in real-time
In a feeding frenzy
Sharks on neurotic overdrive

Saturation

The sponge conspires
One more drop
For self actualization

The drinker drinks
One more drink
To silence the lambs

Urban America sprawls
On Life's grand highway
Toasting its salvation

And the World waits
While bodies strive
To live and breathe

Saturation defines a point
Of mutual equilibrium
A point of no return

War Museum

If war could be a memory
And peace a new world order
Would the world miss its wars?
Would a museum be enough to sustain us?
What is peace without war?

America born from war with England
England born from war with Rome
Rome born from war with Egypt
All civilizations conceived
On the death of war

A war museum, proof of great struggle
Put on display, lest we forget
We are barbarians still
Great evolution we face
Great moral tribulation awaits

And while no one was looking
Japan kicked America's ass
Enter The Bomb
The great equalizer

Which begat super powers and cold wars
Which begat walls and hard lines
Which begat paranoia and terror, still
If only war could end in a museum

Tiny Creatures

In the caves of fertile chemistry
Lurk tiny creatures of protean lust
Cowering and plotting and conspiring
New forms of old destruction
On the life host that feeds and bathes
Their miserable existence
While they wait in ambush for the signal
Like a Martian army of wired idiots
With time and luck in their improbable favor
A mindless force without reason
Broadcasting invisible commands
Of the battle plan
On a field of chaotic biology

Johnny

The lesser child in guilt rises
In time's good grace
And wandered in new culture
Of wonder and contempt
And deep anxiety of conspiracy

You were not chosen
You were a product of the collective disease
In your need for love
A course was set
And into that path was June

In deep prison cells
Souls wondered and waited
On the surface of those days
Citizens heaved a breathe of relief
In the comfort of your song

The man in black
A sinner and a saint
Suffered self-destruction
Overcame with faith
And a dark messages of hope

Crossing the Moral Threshold

Is freedom without bounds?
Or is it bounded by morality?
A separation of culture from chaos
Culture requires a moral threshold
Freedom does not

Cross the moral threshold
Enter a world of the brightest days
And the darkest nights
Angels and vampires at war
Over your soul

Culture Crash

In America worlds collide
You can hear the crashing all around
A Muslim slams a jet plane into a New York
sky scraper
A citizen blasts down a government building
in Oklahoma
A Christian guns down an abortion doctor in
Florida
A black man is beaten by white cops in
California
A white truck driver is beaten by black men
A red man screams like a butterfly in the
desert

In our culture we feel safe
In our cars the world is untouchable
Beyond the safety of our reality
We dream on cruise control
Forgetting the randomness of chaos, Crash!
We all want happiness
But it will cost you
And the crash will set the price

Crashing is the evolution of culture

Alexander

Beneath a Grecian blue sky deep caves of
hidden stories unfold in darkness to a prince of
future kingdoms untold mysteries exposed and
kiss a hungry young spirit ripe with fortunes
want of discovery and execution, as giant
titans and gods of ancient kingdoms reach
through time's eternal thread of theatre for
our entertainment and our hero's
contemplation blasting through walls of ages
to guide both on a journey of death and
conquest one life one village one culture one
continent at a time through blood drenched
trails of pride and loss, a bedlam of freedom's
awakening on Earth's new born awakened
souls speeding towards a redemption of will
and the father's justice while mother works
her magic and hopes and waits for the day her
son will justify her lust of pride and power
over mortals in their pathetic routine, in his
triangle Alexander dreams of a world of east
and west in a coexistence of peace and love
and strength in themselves, while the
underworld conspires the story of the day, a
world that remains divided with hate and
greed of pride's essential demise, of the king's
weakness in his real mortality, Alexander was
great, another painting on the wall, another
down fall.

Nation Rising

A nation rises

Orogeny of primordial consciousness
Building pyramids, gods of decadence
Newton and gravitation
A fall sensation

Ancient sky images disclose the dawn
Cradles of earth-mind dwellers
Living earth, breathing soul
Morning storm precludes the vision
Dispels the dawn
Warring nations
A manifestation of destination

War machines beget the night
The seeds are sown
The souls to reap
Upon the sacred mountain, lies

A child falls

The Goddess of Democracy

May 30, 1989

They raised the statue that spring evening
Half way round the world in another place
They tried and failed
The statue fell and burned
And Moa looked on from beneath the beaten
canvas
As spirits rose from the chaos and clashed
Steel giants on flesh
Crushed the masses
Pen and sword
True Democracy cannot be stopped
The Goddess will have her day
The people will have their way

Storming Rainbows

January 16, 1991

4:50 pm a rainbow formed
The covenant painted on sky
Thoughts turned to dust
And the desert
As ashes fell on old Baghdad

7:00 pm news, the weather looks bad
A desert storm

The world at war in old Babylon
Whirling rainbows begat the world
Storming rainbows beget the end
The cost of freedom
Measured in death and loss

A battle won
But the war rages on

Freedom and Fear

September 11, 2001

Two towers crashed and burned
In a city of giants of freedom
Fear and hate and insanity at war
With America

Within the hours the flag arose
Above the smoke and the flames
Heroes and dead and confusion
But a nation is polarized and sure

Sure of their resilience and faith
In the flag and its symbol and freedom
In God and in country and citizenship
In brotherhood and love and in peace

Our leader is sure and is confident
And we listen and we hope and we pray
For those that are lost and are grieving
And for those that will suffer the justice

Please God bless America
And forgive and heal those that terrorize
And give us the strength and the courage
To free the world of this fear

No End on a Circle

We choose to be the conqueror
To challenge and defeat
To try against infinity
Where justice has no seat

To conquer sky, mountain, water
In a war, a battle slaughter
And in the peace our wounds may heal
For those who lost will never steal

But in their hearts a lust may grow
Desire to stain the fresh new snow
To seek an end on a circle

Trolling the Depths

Wise men troll the depths of knowledge
Seeking patterns of truth in the turmoil of life
While the masses consume the barrage of
effect
Causes obscured by the routine of vice
Become the beacons of faith
And virtue

Where do we begin to comprehend
The complexities of existence
In this madness of dream and illusion?
Where is the kernel of truth
That must be seeded somewhere in ourselves?

If a man lays bare his soul on his sleeve
And sheds the chains of materialism
Will an angel arrive in time
To save him?
Will the grace of brotherhood
Secure his place in the grand story of man?

Are we creatures of annihilation
To be consumed by the fires of Physics
Or a force in this grand universe
For the propagation of the moral good
That we believe exists and we struggle
To secure, hold, and share?

So many religions grapple with this beat
With an agenda to settle this score

And become the psycho-genetic code
Of future generations
At odds with themselves and reality

Where will this search lead us
Where will the struggle end?

Chapter Four:
Celebration

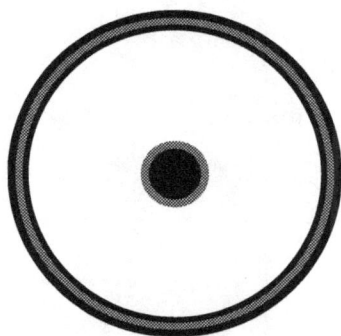

Laughter and Tears

We need comedy to coexist
To break down barriers
To bond in a common positive emotion
To laugh, laughter

We need comedy to laugh at ourselves
At our culture, race, religion
To put these odds on a podium
Create a distance
An objective perspective
The comedy in our tragedy on parade

Humor is a positive agent
In our quest for freedom
Peaceful coexistence

Humor is a requirement
For evolution and survival
A characteristic of intelligent life

In the end
All will be one big chorus
Of laughter and tears of joy

Keep On Truckin'

Cultures celebrate life's great events
And death's dark doors
In pitiful throes to reason
With the guilt that feeds
On troubled and shaken souls

In ironic reasoning to justify the self
To secure the passage
To plant the seed
To honor and acknowledge
Cultures mobilize the courage to move on

Time and mortality fund and cast lives
The silent producer and director
Of an endless movie
On the grand highway

Cultures celebrate life's great events
And muster the courage to move on

Unstoppable Life

As the Earth turns another corner
And the Sun creeps a little more each day
And the winds bring new warmth
And rain
Unstoppable life returns

No stopping the buds and the leaves
All around unstoppable life breeds
Consuming the death of old decay
Reaching into the Earth
Transforming energy
Pushing into the sky
Exhausting our breath
A sacrifice for our consumption

In the desert of the universe
A spec of blue and green spins
An oasis of unstoppable life
As the winter time ends

Spring Time

My favorite time is Spring
The soft rains and thirsty ground
Meet to produce colorful things
In great abundance all around

As the geese of winter thaw and build nests
As the trees of winter warm in new sunshine
As the creatures locked in winter's grip spring
free
As the Earth and the Sun conspire another
Spring time

Human thought wanders and wonders
Of new beginnings and possibilities
Primal urges surge and plant themselves
Waiting for the right moment

Full throttle tires smoke
Squealing out at Spring's presence
A smoking proclamation of urgency
In boredom and want

Of meat and machine

Celebration of the Bus

It's a right of passage to ride the bus. In the randomness of our lives, paths cross and connections are made for the moment then break and fade. The Bus.

At the stop, waiting, wondering what the ride will bring, memories emerge and merge with the moment, forming pools of now and then and tomorrow and it's all exciting and hum drum together. At the stop we wonder and wait.

Waiting for the bus. Glances exchanged. Judgments made and reconsidered. Do I have the right change? Look at that! I'm too fat. Maybe I should get that.

It's the same and different every time. A jungle cruise in a bus. The diversity of the fauna from ride to ride rivals the depths of the deepest rain forest. All age, economic, and ethnic groups are sampled, stored, and packed tight. Move it to the back. To the back of the bus.

A thought, a touch, a glance, a new view, an old sound in a new direction, a loud encounter, a cold ride, a funny sight, a strange smell, a song pouring out of hot bodies ripe in vacation's sunny side, deep laughter in light

65

humor wanting human interaction and acceptance.

In the bus we celebrate and rejoice in the freedom of our vacation.

The Point of Music

The point of music is simple
It's a connection
A communication
From cell to cell
Connecting life
Through rhythmic sound waves

Sounds traverse the emptiness
Carrying and distributing energy
To matter existing in the void of space
In a random mathematical happening
Music is an equation of this random math
That courses through our cells

In a vibration celebration

Over Your Head

Summer is the time to jump in, to live and to breathe in your freedom and your love of the moment, of your life, of your celebration of being you in today, just breathe, and know that now is your time, a time that no one else can claim, it's yours and it's real for you and for your existence, it is ripe and it needs you to swim the race of your life, to win, to be confident of the skin that you're in, to take that dare, to bust down those walls sheltering your insecurities, to lower your defenses and raise your offenses, to challenge tomorrow despite today, to be you today, to define your tomorrow, to love yourself today, to hate yourself some other day, that may never be.

Jump in over your head and swim.

Wasted

I am solid
No anticipation
I know the score
I am fine with my sense
Of what will be
And then
Shit happens

I am ready
Ready for the score
Anticipation of a happening
Choices presented
Decisions made
But then
No happening

Sometimes shit happens
And sometimes shit doesn't happen
Either way it's shitty

Failure in destiny
Lost opportunity in free will
Two hands dig deep
Into the waste
And feel warm
In the cesspool
Of freedom's revelry

The Concert

Singular in a crowd
Sudden darkness
Silence ready to erupt
Anticipation
Wonder and a warm feeling
A heavy breath held
Eyes and ears aligned

Beat, beat, beat, bam, bam, beat, beat, CLASH
BRIGHT LIGHTS
Flicker and fade
Beat, beat, bam, BAM
CLASH
Electric fingers play

Rush of signals
Visual and acoustic overload
Floor pushing
Crowd pulling
The air rocking and rolling

Momentum and rhythm
Hold and carry
Merging the one
With the many

An arena of perception contrived
For pleasure from the pain
A rock and roll insane

Friday Night

A cold beer by my side
And a snappy tune on the video
Mars shining bright
The world captured and full of its new gravity
It's been 60,000 years.

My beer tastes good
And my heart beats to the tune
Of the night
I am alive
Tonight

Smells Like Life

Today I lived another day
Tomorrow I'll live again
This flatulence
It touches me
A warm and friendly hand

The artist is at once the art
And life is once the artist
Painting scenes of copralites
Embryonic, libido baker

Stellar Observations

Hell hath no fury like a culture in birth
Said the giant to the nimble elf
Dancing in the moonlight on a cold summer
day
Wrapped in a funeral amazement of stars
Rocking, rolling in all directions
Touching moonbeams
Stealing through the mind's eye
Small observations
Of a stellar birth
An alignment of will and stars
The creation of a new world culture
The grand unification
Of peace, love, and humanity

The Arts

Have you seen your reflection on the page?

In the child's painting, House on the Hill,
Mother and Father?

In the tall sleek glass skyscrapers in the city,
in a blade of grass?

In an instant thrown from eternity,
into the womb of humanity.

All around us, images, confirmation of
reservation
displace the illusion and fill the void.

Caught between two worlds, born to sin, living
for death,
searching for answers, for teachers, for
friends.

A brotherhood of understanding, of suffering,
of retribution and salvation.

Flowers grow strong and bright from the
waste.

Have you seen yourself in the arts?

Beat Rhapsody

In one voice the world sings a troubling song
Building a cadence that breaks spirits
And builds prisons
In many songs the singer tells a brave story
Opening eyes that see the injustice
And frees slaves

It's hard to aim true with cloudy vision and
vapor targets
To eliminate the obvious and search for the
forgotten
The apple of the fall
To forget the deal in the garden
Searching for an excuse to exist
To get the point

In this labyrinth of injustice and chaos
A disease of all the ages
Sitting pretty in our home
A home that we have created in our great
wisdom
In our passion for mediocrity
We wait for a brave hero
To deliver

WAKE UP!

Mortality is the transient happening of flesh
and soul
The rest is just a cherished picture

Anything else is just a bet with time

Polonius offered a fine gift to those with an
open ear.
Can you, above all, be true to yourself?

Dig your own beat.

Independence Day

"We hold these truths to be self-evident, that all men are created equal, that they are endowed by their Creator with certain unalienable Rights that among these are Life, Liberty, and the pursuit of Happiness. — That to secure these rights, Governments are instituted among Men, deriving their just powers from the consent of the governed, — That whenever any Form of Government becomes destructive of these ends, it is the Right of the People to alter or to abolish it, and to institute new Government, laying its foundation on such principles and organizing its powers in such form, as to them shall seem most likely to effect their Safety and Happiness."

— Committee of Five